eacher's friend publications

Reproduci for Early Learners!

MW00700800

Little Kids... DRAW!

Simple Patterns for Developing Drawing and Writing Skills!

Written and Illustrated by:
Karen Sevaly
Contributing Editor:
Libby Perez
Graphic Designer:
Cory Jackson

Look for All of Our Little Kids... Books
at your local educational retailer!

Table of Contents

Copyright © 2000
Teacher's Friend, a Scholastic Company.
All rights reserved.
Printed in China.

ISBN-13 978-0-439-54955-4
ISBN-10 0-439-54955-8

Safety Warning! The activities and patterns in this book are appropriate for children age 3 to 6 years old. It is important that children only use materials and products labeled child-safe and non-toxic. Remember that young children should always be supervised by a competent adult and youngsters must never be allowed to put small objects or art materials in their mouths. Please consult the manufacturer's safety warnings on all materials and equipment used with young children.

Little Kids...
Books!

Welcome to the wonderful world of
young learners where play is learning
and learning is fun!

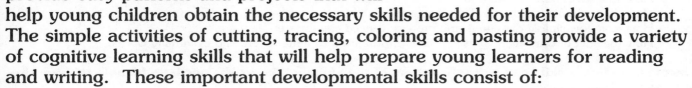

With these *Little Kids...Books!*, teachers can
provide easy patterns and projects that will
help young children obtain the necessary skills needed for their development.
The simple activities of cutting, tracing, coloring and pasting provide a variety
of cognitive learning skills that will help prepare young learners for reading
and writing. These important developmental skills consist of:

Fine Motor Skills
> finger-wrist dexterity, arm-hand movement, eye-hand coordination

Perceptual Motor Skills
> identification, color and shape recognition, matching and location,
> spatial relationships

Expressive and Receptive Language Skills
> listening, speaking, questioning, relating words and pictures,
> imitation, utilization, recognition and discrimination, visual
> perception and discrimination

Social and Emotional Skills
> creativity and imagination, pride in accomplishments, self-reliance,
> self-control, self-confidence

The early years of schooling helps determine how a child will learn for a life-
time. During this period, children develop a sense of self and decide whether
school is a burden or a joy. We hope these books assist you in your goal to
provide each child with a fulfilling and fun learning experience!

Introduction

Little Kids...Draw!

The art center in your classroom should be filled with a variety of art materials that offer children the opportunity to experiment with colors, shapes, textures and designs. Drawing, painting and making art projects benefit all aspects of a child's development. Through art, children can express how they think, feel and relate to the world around them. The materials used should provide a wide range of opportunity for imagination, discovery and experimentation. In most cases these art experiences need to be purely creative and not restrictive to a child's imagination and individuality.

However, as small children develop their fine motor skills and eye-hand coordination, drawing specific shapes and designs can be introduced as a means to ready a child for reading and writing. The tracing and drawing patterns found in this book will help young learners develop their fine and perceptual motor skills needed for beginning writing. These patterns and pages have been designed to help teach young learners in the following ways:
- How to draw simple shapes and follow a given line
- How these shapes can be used to draw animals, objects, designs, etc.
- How to follow simple directions and more advanced step-by-step directions.
- How the skill of drawing shapes and lines can be used to write letters and eventually words.

Remember, before a child can write the letters of the alphabet, he or she needs to be able to draw simple lines and basic shapes.

While using this book, you can help foster each child's creativity by encouraging him or her to expand their artistic talents beyond the given patterns. For example: Suggest that the children draw the cat's tail any length they wish. Or, encourage them to color the cat their favorite color. How about purple polka dots!

HOLDING A PENCIL/CRAYON CORRECTLY - Young children will naturally tend to hold a crayon or pencil in their fist. Gently show children how they have more control, if they hold the pencil similar to that of the second illustration. You may find that each child holds a pencil in a way that best fits his or her hand naturally. (Remember, some children have short fingers and others have long.) Simply encourage a balanced, relaxed grip. Very young children may tend to use either hand when first drawing. Usually by five years old, the dominant hand is well established. Authorities agree that there is no merit in attempting to make a left-handed child to use his or her right hand.

NO!   **YES!**

FIRST TIME DRAWING ACTIVITIES - Before children can trace a given line, they need experience at simple freehand drawing. You will find that youngsters love to draw and experiment with different writing tools, colors and surfaces. Here are some fun suggestions that will enhance their development:
- Have each child draw using large-sized crayons (with paper peeled away) on an extra large sheet of butcher paper taped to the classroom floor.
- Instead of asking children to draw specific items, ask them to draw something happy, funny, pretty, etc. Encourage the children to attempt various methods of creativity and self-expression.
- Have students practice drawing on a vertical surface by attaching a large sheet of paper to an easel, wall, door or outside fence. This will enable them to exercise the muscles in their fingers and hands in a different way.
- Provide a sand table or large dishpan filled with clean sand and have students draw designs and shapes using their fingers or plastic utensils. (You may want to add water to the sand and have the children draw in wet sand as well.)
- On a warm, sunny day, give students a cup of clean water and a paint brush and encourage them to draw on the sidewalk or block wall. Food coloring can be added to the water for extra fun.
- Place several dollops of shaving cream on a cookie sheet. Have the child smooth out the shaving cream and then draw in the cream with a pointed index finger.
- You can also cover a cookie sheet with chocolate pudding. Make sure the child has clean hands before drawing the designs and instruct him or her to not lick their fingers until after the exercise.
- Cover an 8 inch square of cardboard with aluminum foil and have the child draw on the foil using a blunt pencil or craft stick.

Note: Before using the tracing patterns in this book, make sure the children understand that they are to follow the direction of the arrows indicated on the pages. To illustrate the significance of the arrows you may want to draw arrows in four directions on the chalkboard--right, left, up and down. Have students point in the direction each arrow points. Children can also draw a chalk line from the arrow on the board to the direction in which it points.

FIRST TIME DRAWING ACTIVITIES - After significant practice at drawing on their own, you can now begin introducing the patterns in this book.   Here are a few helpful hints:

- **Crayons Not Pencils** - Have the children use crayons rather than pencils with beginning tracing and drawing activities. Large crayons with the paper removed are easier for small hands to hold and manipulate.
- **Lines** - In most cases encourage children to draw vertical lines top to bottom and horizontal lines left to right. In this way, children will later be able to transfer their tracing and drawing abilities into the writing of letters, numbers and words.
- **Shapes** - By drawing shapes, children can begin to draw objects and things rather than just squiggles.

Suggested Materials for the Early Childhood Art Center

PAPER

drawing paper	construction paper
cardboard	butcher paper
newsprint	craft paper
crepe paper	finger paint paper
tracing paper	newspaper
tissue paper	wallpaper
wrapping paper	cellophane
paper plates	manila paper
waxed paper	cupcake liners

GLUE

white household glue (in plastic squeeze bottles, non-toxic)
glue sticks

MISC. MATERIALS

crayons	chalk
clay	felt-tip pens
rulers	scissors (blunt ends)
rubber bands	hole punch
paper tubes	egg cartons
clothespins	paper lunch sacks
baby food jars	stapler and staples
shoe boxes	coffee cans
margarine tubs	hangers
drinking straws	paper cups
cellophane tape	plastic wrap
plastic bottles	stamp pads & stamps

CLEAN UP

paper towels	newspapers
sponges	anti-bacterial soap
student smocks	

PAINT

tempera paint   finger paint
watercolor paint

PAINT ACCESSORIES

1 inch wide flat bristle brushes
Size 4-6 (pointed) camel hair watercolor brushes
Size 6-12 (round) camel hair or bristle brushes
sponges (various sizes and shapes)
paint rollers

DECORATIVE MATERIALS

Natural Things

seeds	nuts	beads
shells	feathers	dried beans
acorns	pine cones	pebbles

Fabrics

burlap	corduroy	cotton gingham
felt	fake fur	lace
terry cloth	denim	canvas

Building Things

nails	tiles	wood scraps
linoleum	wire mesh	wire
sandpaper		

Decorations

buttons	glitter	gummed stars
stickers	confetti	colored tape
sequins	tin foil	cotton balls
corks	paper clips	dried macaroni
string	yarn	popsicle sticks
styrofoam	toothpicks	pipe cleaners
ribbons		

Please Remember! It is important that children only use materials and products labeled child-safe and non-toxic. Remember that young children should always be supervised by a competent adult and youngsters must never be allowed to put small objects or art materials in their mouths. Please consult the manufacturer's safety warnings on all materials and equipment you use with young children.

I Can Draw! Step-By-Step Directions!

Patterns can be found on pages 34-48.

LEARNING ESSENTIAL SKILLS WITH STEP-BY-STEP DRAWING PATTERNS
The step-by-step drawing pages offer young learners a fun way to practice a variety of essential skills. These skills include:

      fine motor skills - finger-wrist dexterity, eye-hand coordination
      perceptual motor skills - shape recognition, matching and location, sequencing and spatial relations
      expressive language skills - questioning, imitation, utilization, visual perception
      social and emotional skills - pride in accomplishments, self-reliance, self-confidence

DEVELOPMENTAL DRAWING
Drawings that a child creates himself/herself is known as "developmentally appropriate art." "Dictated art" consists of art projects that require children to follow a set pattern. The step-by-step patterns found in this book represent a type of "dictated art."

Children experience four specific drawing stages as they learn to use simple art materials. Very young children will at first only scribble in a disorganized way. Later this scribbling will become more controlled. As the child progresses in development he will give his pictures names even though the drawings are unrecognizable. And lastly, the young child will draw pictures representing a specific object or scene. It is during this later stage, and only when the child shows interest in making their drawings look more "grown-up," that the "step-by-step directions" pages should be introduced. Not all young learners will be ready to follow the step-by-step directions, but most four and five year olds will enjoy making a simple shape transform into a cute animal or object.

ENCOURAGE CREATIVITY
Encourage each child to be creative in modeling the simple step-by-step drawings by choosing unusual colors, varying the size or by adding details. You could also have the children cut their pictures out and paste them to large sheets of colored construction paper. Each child can then draw their own background or enhancements to their original drawings.

IDEAS ON USING THESE PATTERNS IN YOUR ART CENTER
   1. Laminate the step-by-step patterns for durability and keep them for children to use again and again.
   2. Select three or four step-by-step patterns to keep in your center. Let each child choose one of the
       pages to model into their own creation using supplied colored paper, crayons, markers, etc.
   3. With more advanced students, make copies of the patterns and have them available for individual use.
       The child can duplicate the drawing of box 6 in the other five boxes. Encourage the child to color
       each drawing differently or alter the drawings in different ways.
   4. More advanced students may also like to cut the step-by-step directions apart and then paste them in
       sequence to a larger sheet of paper.

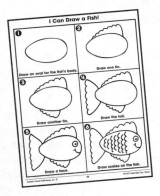
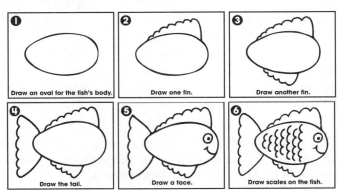

TF1457 Little Kids...Dr

I can Draw!

_____
Name

_____   _____
Teacher   Date

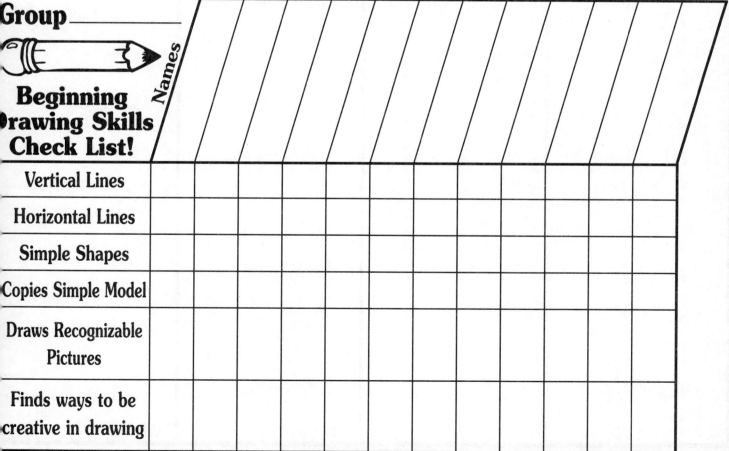

Group _____

Beginning Drawing Skills Check List!

	Names									
Vertical Lines										
Horizontal Lines										
Simple Shapes										
Copies Simple Model										
Draws Recognizable Pictures										
Finds ways to be creative in drawing										

Trace and draw these lines.

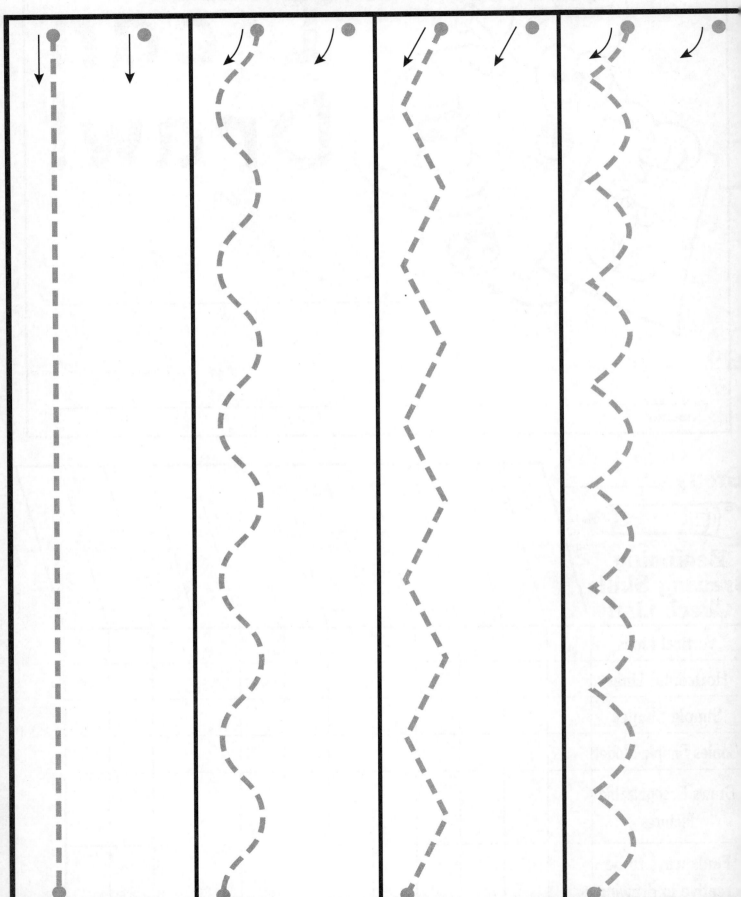

8

TF1457 Little Kids...Dr

Trace and draw these lines.

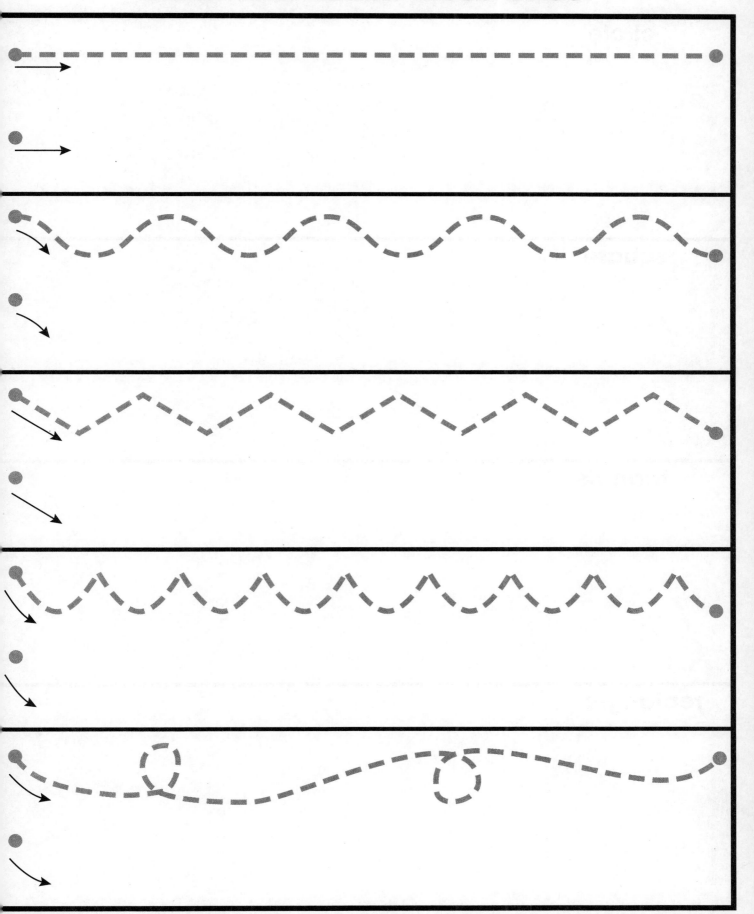

Trace, complete and draw these shapes.

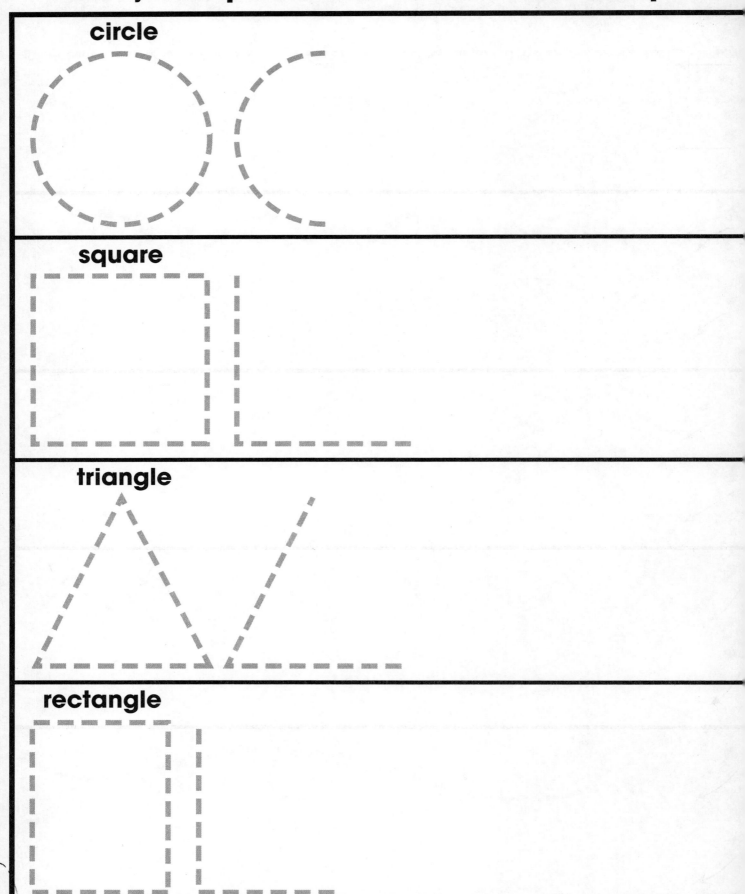

circle

square

triangle

rectangle

TF1457 Little Kids...Dra

Trace, complete and draw these shapes.

oval

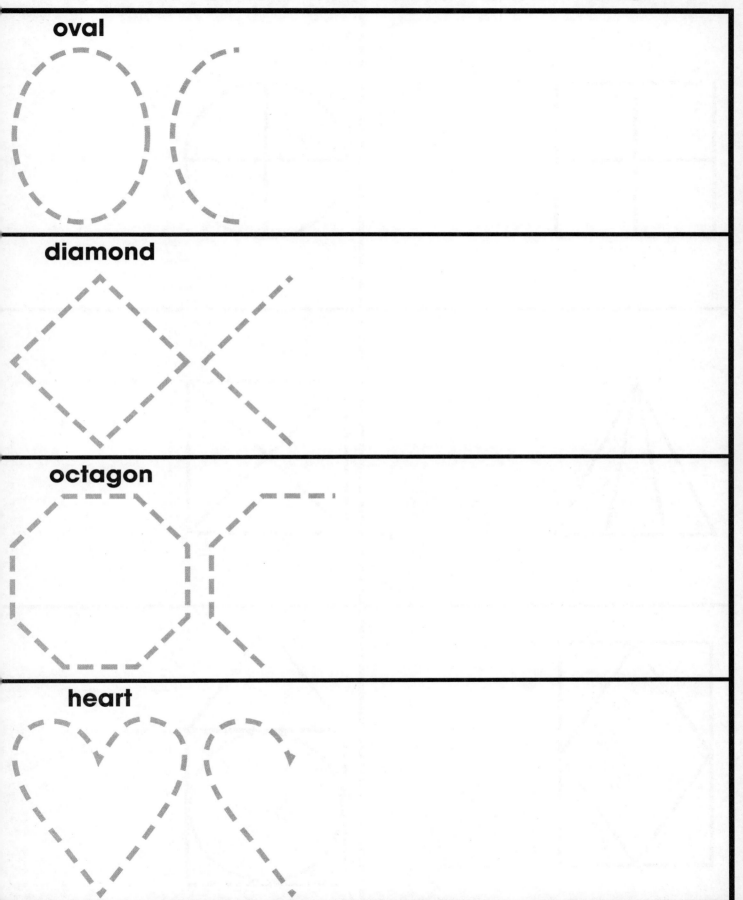

diamond

octagon

heart

Complete the second shape to look like the first one

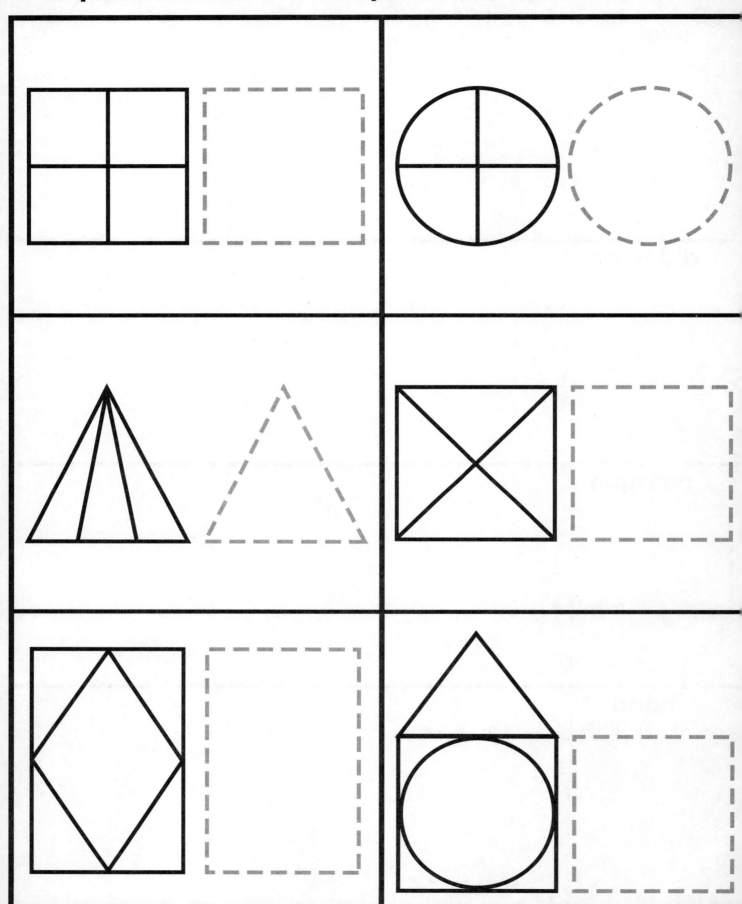

Complete the second shape to look like the first one.

Trace and color this sun. Draw a face.

Trace and color this snowman. Draw a face.

Trace and color this gingerbread man. Draw a face.

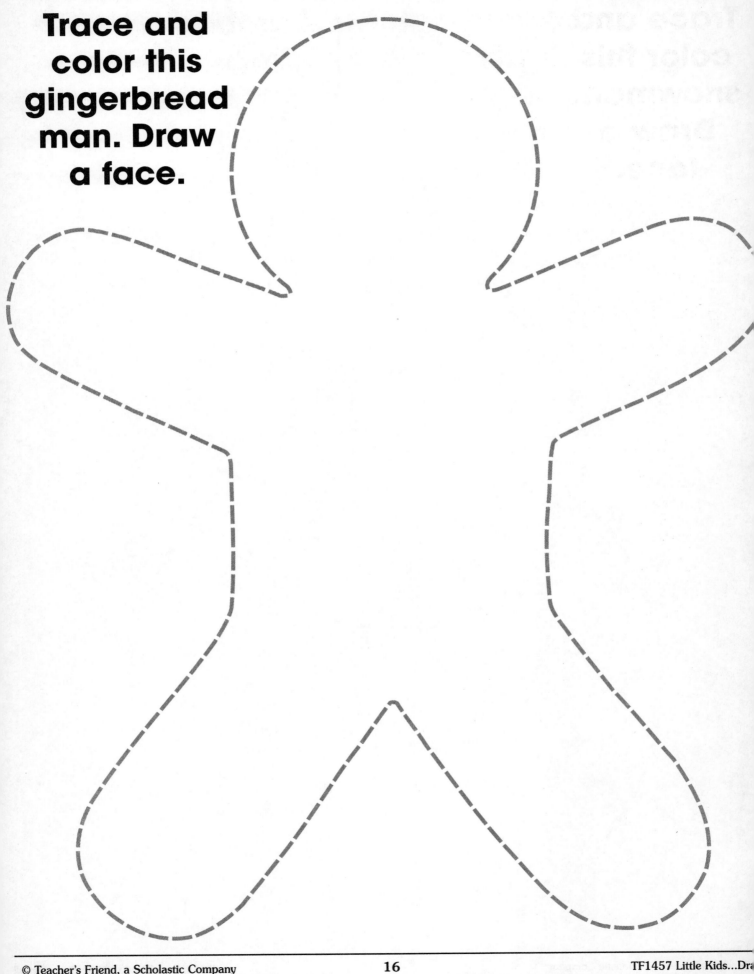

TF1457 Little Kids...Dra

Trace and color this umbrella.
Draw some raindrops.

TF1457 Little Kids...Draw!

Trace and color this whale.
Draw his spout.

TF1457 Little Kids...Dra

Help this boy draw a picture. Color the boy.

Draw what's in this fishbowl. Color the girl.

Draw what is outside this window.

Draw a face on this pumpkin. Color the cat.

Draw this turkey's tail feathers.
Color the turkey.

Draw presents under this tree and the tree's decorations. Color the tree.

TF1457 Little Kids...Dra

What is growing?
Color the girl.

Draw what is in this nest. Color the bird and nest.

Draw what this boy is thinking.
Color the boy.

Draw what is in the sky.
Color the scene.

28

TF1457 Little Kids...Dra

Draw what this diver sees. Color the diver.

Draw this clown's balloons.
Color the clown.

Draw what is in this treasure chest.
Color the chest.

Draw a face. Color the face.

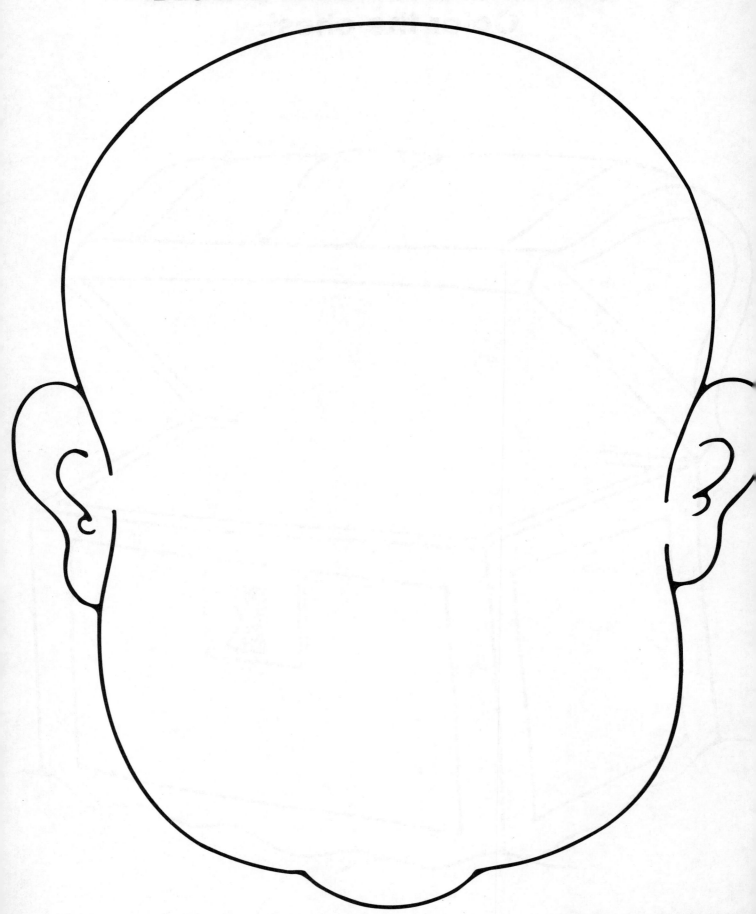

32

Decorate this cake. Color the cake.

I Can Draw a Cat!

① Draw a circle for the cat's head.

② Draw the cat's body.

③ Draw 2 ears.

④ Draw a tail.

⑤ Draw a cute face.

⑥ Draw the cat's whiskers.

TF1457 Little Kids...Dr

I Can Draw a Flower!

1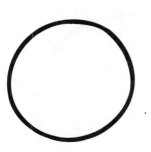

Draw a circle.

2

Draw small petals around the circle.

3

Draw large petals.

4

Draw two leaves.

5

Draw a cute face.

6

Color your flower.

I Can Draw a Turtle!

1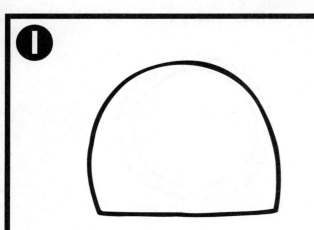

Draw the turtle's shell.

2

Draw the head and neck.

3

Draw four feet.

4

Draw a cute face.

5

Draw the toes.

6

Draw designs on the turtle's shell.

I Can Draw a Snake!

 1

Draw a pair of eyes.

 2

Draw the snake's body and head.

 3

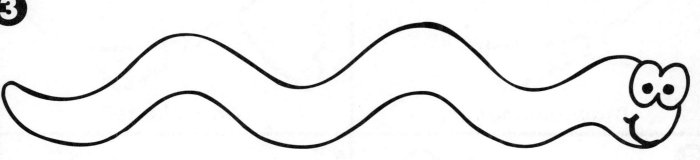

Draw a face.

 4

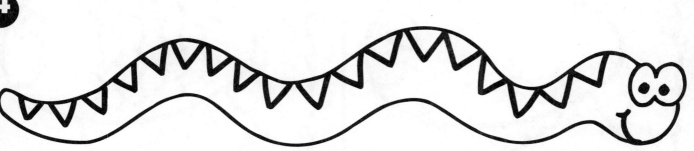

Draw designs on the snake.

I Can Draw a Fish!

①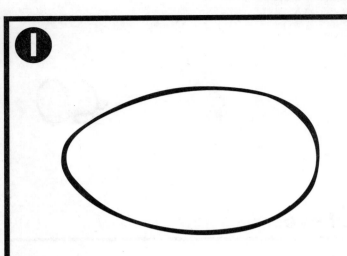

Draw an oval for the fish's body.

②

Draw one fin.

③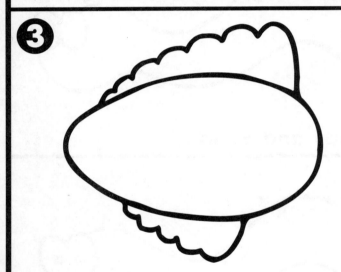

Draw another fin.

④

Draw the tail.

⑤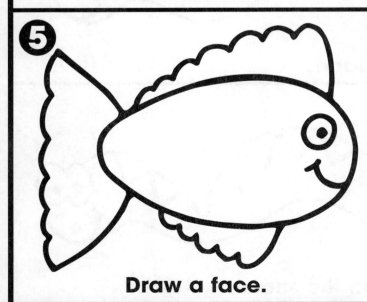

Draw a face.

⑥

Draw scales on the fish.

TF1457 Little Kids...Dr

I Can Draw a Horse!

 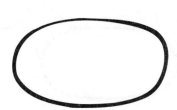

Draw an oval for the horse's body.

Draw the head and neck.

Draw the four legs.

Draw a face and two ears.

Draw a mane and tail.

Draw a saddle.

I Can Draw a Reindeer!

1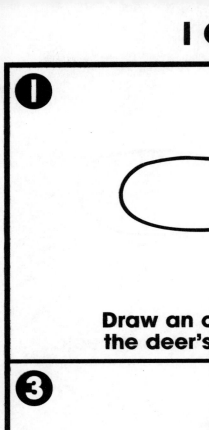

Draw an oval for the deer's body.

2

Draw the head and neck.

3

Draw two ears.

4

Draw four legs.

5

Draw the deer's tail, eyes and nose.

6

Draw the deer's antlers.

I Can Draw a Turkey!

1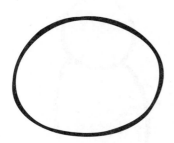

Draw an oval for the turkey's body.

2

Draw the neck and head.

3

Draw and eye and beak.

4

Draw the turkey's wattle.

5

Draw the tail feathers.

6

Draw the turkey's feet.

I Can Draw a Bee!

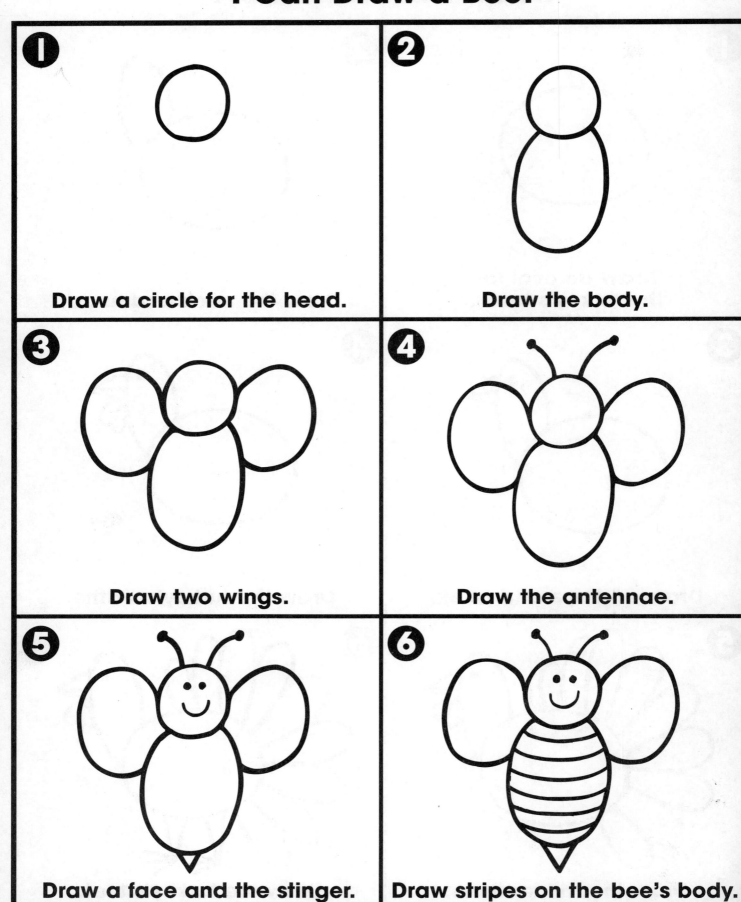

1 Draw a circle for the head.

2 Draw the body.

3 Draw two wings.

4 Draw the antennae.

5 Draw a face and the stinger.

6 Draw stripes on the bee's body.

TF1457 Little Kids...Dr

I Can Draw a Bunny!

1 Draw a circle for the bunny's head.

2 Draw the bunny's body.

3 Draw the front feet.

4 Draw the ears.

5 Draw a fluffy tail.

6 Draw a cute face.

I Can Draw a Elephant!

①
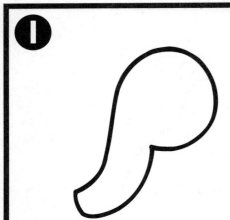

Draw the elephant's head and trunk.

②

Draw his ears.

③

Draw his body.

④

Draw his four legs.

⑤

Draw a cute face.

⑥

Draw his toes and tail.

I Can Draw a Teddy Bear!

1 Draw a circle for the teddy bear's head.

2 Draw a body.

3 Draw the ears.

4 Draw the arms and legs.

5 Draw a cute face.

6 Color the teddy bear.

I Can Draw a Frog!

1 Draw an oval for the frog's body.

2 Draw two small circles for the eyes.

3 Draw the frog's eyes and mouth.

4 Draw the back legs.

5 Draw the front legs.

6 Color the frog.

TF1457 Little Kids...Dr

I Can Draw a Christmas Tree!

Draw the top of your tree.

Draw the second layer of branches.

Draw the third layer of branches.

Draw the fourth layer of branches.

Draw the tree's trunk.

Color and decorate the Christmas Tree.

I Can Draw a Butterfly!

1

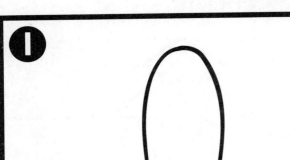

Draw an oval for the butterfly's body.

2

Draw two wings.

3

Draw two more wings.

4

Draw the antennae.

5

Draw a cute face.

6

Draw your own designs on the butterfly's wings. Color your butterfly.